POETRY BOOKS BY YAEL S. HACOHEN

The Dove That Didn't Return, 2024

Between Sanctity and Sand, 2021

The Dove That Didn't Return

Poems by

Yael S. Hacohen

HOLY COW! PRESS
Duluth, Minnesota
2024

Cover image created by Daniel Goldfarb.
Author photograph by Doron Letzler.
Book and cover design by Anton Khodakovsky.

Printed and bound in the United States.
First printing, Spring, 2024.
10 9 8 7 6 5 4 3 2 1

Library of Congress Cataloging-in-Publication Data
Hacohen, Yael, 1986- author.
The dove that didn't return / poems by Yael Hacohen.
Dove that didn't return (Compilation) | Dove that did not return
[Duluth] : Holy Cow! Press, 2024.
LCCN 2023031868 | ISBN 9781737405191 (trade paperback)
LCSH: War poetry. | LCGFT: Poetry.
LCC PS3608.A2558 D68 2024 | DDC 811/.6--dc23/eng/20231016
LC record available at https://lccn.loc.gov/2023031868

Holy Cow! Press projects are funded in part by grant awards from the
Ben and Jeanne Overman Charitable Trust, the Elmer L. and Eleanor J.
Andersen Foundation, the Lenfestey Family Foundation, the Woessner
Freeman Family Foundation and by gifts from generous individual
donors. We are grateful to Springboard for the Arts for their support
as our fiscal sponsor.

Holy Cow! Press books are distributed to the trade by Consortium
Book Sales & Distribution, c/o Ingram Publisher Services, Inc., 210
American Drive, Jackson, TN 38301.

For inquiries, please write to: *Holy Cow! Press*, Post Office Box 3170,
Mount Royal Station, Duluth, MN 55803.
Visit *www.holycowpress.org*

Uri, who teaches me peace.

"But the dove found no resting place for the sole of her foot, and she returned into the ark to him, for the waters were on the face of the whole earth. So he put out his hand and took her, and drew her into the ark to himself. And he waited yet another seven days, and again he sent the dove out from the ark. Then the dove came to him in the evening, and behold, a freshly plucked olive leaf was in her mouth; and Noah knew that the waters had receded from the earth. So he waited yet another seven days and sent out the dove, which did not return again to him anymore." (Gen. 8:9-12, King James Version)

TABLE OF CONTENTS

I

GENESIS

— *"After every war / someone has to clean up."*
Wisława Szymborska

What Szymborska didn't say:
that someone is always you.
No one is coming.

No headline article, no volunteers with blankets.
No cleaners in vans or officials with flowers.
You will have to shimmy up and go in and scrub off the gore.

Separate the fingers from the pieces of glass.
They'll be your fingers.
They'll be your friend's fingers.

And you'll have to find a cloth and run
the cloth in hot water. And the water will burn,
or you won't even feel it. You'll have to quiet

everyone into a building and stay very still.
It'll be hours or years while the manhunt defers.
And no one will offer a road or a stitch of a road.

You'll be twenty-five, sweat dripping through
your hair bun, your vest, your helmet,
and you'll march with the squadron.

That's when you'll know that cleaning
is not even the start, not even the bud
of the start, of what you'll have to do.

BETWEEN SANCTITY AND SAND

The first time I shot an M-16
it was the heat of summer in the Negev.
Gas-operated with a rotating bolt, five-point-fifty-
six caliber, with nineteen bullets a box.
I could shoot like an angel.
I could hit a running target
at six-hundred-fifty meters.
I hummed to myself as I shot,
I was eighteen.
The retama flower of my hair-bun drawn back tight
blooming, sprouting open with every green round.

AND YET THE SEA ISN'T FULL

Count them, the Kippahs in the Synagogue.
My mother folds games for me in the hem of her skirt.
My hand & hers bound together like the leather straps of the Tefillin.

How about this, she whispers.
See if you can find an orange one.

I peer over the railing of the women's section
of the Synagogue but his Kippah is hidden
like the curtain that conceals the tangerine Torah Scrolls.

Can you spot Abba? In the sea of men
who all look alike, my father is a small wave
I recognize from any lighthouse.

He seems far, and I press into her like sand.
This is the most important part, she says.
When the Shofar blows, you can wish for peace.

But when I hear the horn,
only missile-boats come to mind.

SHACHARIT

It's Sunday morning in Tel Aviv.
It's winter but the days are still

desert long. The house echoes and bows
as I sit patiently in the kitchen.

waiting for my parents to wake
and get the Frosted Flakes down

from the top shelf I can't reach
even if I stand on my tippy toes.

My parents are still asleep,
and I've been waiting for what feels

like a century. I can't even tell time,
not yet, but I know it must be at least

06:00, because my mother's whole
big terracotta kitchen has its eyes opened

wide and it's already breaking a sweat.
I flip through the dials on my father's old

transistor radio. I hear Arik Einstein's
Yoshev B'SanFranzisco Al HaMayim,

right when he whistles through the lead-in
to the chorus. I can't be more

than six years old, but even then, I think
it's a song out of a different time.

A time before my parents. A time
when the Kibbutz was moral,

when women wore their hair in long braids
parted to the side, when men walked barefoot

and whistled as they worked the land.
There was care then, and a meal

was a thin slice of brown bread
with some butter or salty cheese, and tea

was served boiling in very thin glass cups.
My father was born right after that time,

in 1959, when the sun starting setting
on those ideals and those beautiful thick braids.

The radio broadcaster interrupts
the song right when Arik lets his voice

trail off—right after he sings the line
about rubbing his eyes on the blue. *It's 6:20,*

December 13, 1992, the broadcaster says,
A squad of Hamas militants kidnapped Sergeant

Nissim Toledano from outside his home.

I cannot wait for the broadcaster

to stop talking, I don't understand how
he can interrupt such a great song. Right then,

my father walks into the terracotta kitchen
and puts the tea kettle on. He's wearing

his uniform. Suddenly surprised to see me
sitting there, he exclaims, *Yalulu!* (that's me),

and I cut him off. *Abba,* I say, *I'm just waiting
for the Frosted Flakes.* My father curls his brows

inward, like a warning. He says, *Yael,
never ask for help if you can do it yourself.*

*Now, go get a chair to stand on
from the other room.* And I do, and I don't

argue because, because it's war and the days
are desert long and I don't like waiting

for the broadcaster to stop talking,
for the song to finish, for my father to finally walk in.

THE FIRST TIME ROCKETS FALL IN TEL AVIV

Uri isn't home. I run outside to see. *Clink*, the soft betrayal
of the door locking behind me. Fire ran along
the ground. Sirens mutter prayers.
I'm on my knees. *Please door, let me in, please.*

GHETTO WARSAW

Yosef and His Mighty Coat of Stripes

It was the night he dreamt of baskets
of bread hanging from the trees,
and there it was in the Great Square —
a woman's body swollen and black
with two potatoes still in her hand.

MY FLOCK

—*after Denise Levertov*

All night I watched the bombs fly through the dark sky
like formations of red-beaked egrets, missing my window
over & over.
                    Exploding from sky to sky, their wings
clipped frantically at the edges
of embers. Desperate, their war cry
sounded more
or less.

PILLAR OF CLOUD

If your Personal Number starts with 619
you were drafted in July,
in the heat of a teenage summer,
and you didn't know what to wear

to a drafting. You didn't know
what to do with your arms, almost
dangling like loose strings off a cotton shirt.
You figure the cotton will soak up the sweat,

but you don't know anything
about wind. You don't know
how a lizard hunches over a boulder,
how African ants descent on a corpse

in formation, how the M-16 will bruise
the bow of your shoulder. And you'll move
so many rocks from one tent to another,
for no particular reason if not to teach you

that you don't matter at all.
You are not even a pawn. Not even
the beginning of a number. And the CO
doesn't want to be here; she doesn't like

the swearing. She's going to be a biologist;
she prefers to study small cell carcinomas.
But she understands the way a unit
organizes. She understands an order.

And you will come to understand
that many things she tells you,
will be a kind of truth, though not
a Cicerian truth or an Augustinian truth.

An Old Testament truth is a very long road,
which leads to many paths, and the road
has gravel on it, and offers little shade,
few places to take cover if you hear a shot.

You should know, if your number starts with 619,
you must find your own olive tree. Your own truth,
your own kind of country from which an ancient
prayer may escape your lips and nothing more.

I PULL THE PIN

out of the grenade. I can feel
its dead weight. It's nothing

like holding a rock.
It's like holding a snake

alive in olive green.
A danger containing more

than itself. Of course,
the thing slithers out of my hand

(in a tilting bird kind
of excitement). Everywhere

thorns and thistles.
My CO's helmet hammers

into my shoulder, knocking me down.
It's then, I step into the boots

of my own breath. It's then
my eyes open, and I watch him

become weightless, a single feather
floating, no—flaming, in midair.

SETTLEMENT

I am ordered to evacuate this family by force.
                It's then, I remember a line

of olive trees in a field when I lift
                the shield over my brow.

The shield is like the nation, heavy
                & unlike the nation, I watch

as the husband holds onto the frame
                of the door with his fingertips.

I have never even seen
                a man cry, let alone.

I am told this is for peace
                & when the son crashes

into my shield, I do not
                back down. I advance

sideways, or with a different shade
                of Judaism. I push

my right leg forward & the line
                of my men & women

quickly closes ranks. Not even
                a piece of parchment

could fit between us. These men
                & women are my brothers.

I would die for them, if ordered.
                    I am told this land

has always belonged to Palestine.
                    These are their fields,

their olive trees. No Israeli can live here.
                    I recall the wife

attempting to approach our line.
                    She says, we speak the same

flag, she & I. She ties a ribbon
                    to my shield & I do not

remove it. No Israeli can
                    live here, they tell me.

I raise the shield as if to protect her
                    before ramming it into

the side of her face. My line
                    of men & women

has my back always,
                    & they tell me so.

The husband sees this
                    & releases the wooden frame.

He bends into a question
                    on the ground.

GO INTO DARKNESS

Along the patrol route, the green-purple birds
of sunrise infringe on the desert, the way
a soldier can be a Soldier only
if she acts like a man. Only if she is a man
even when she is not. I shuffle my boots under the weight
of this mundane. The day-to-day boredom
of walking from point Aleph to point Beit.
The brutal sound time makes when it passes.
How to be fatigued like a woman?
I am nineteen, and I am a commander.
I have accomplished everything
and nothing.

Is this the city   I was created for?

I am like Helen of Troy, the static of my hands
undoing the blond feathers of my braid,
taking it apart, wisp by wisp,
only to redo it.

I NEVER SAW A WILD THING SORRY FOR ITSELF

When your CO singles you out in Krav Maga,
you'd better throw a punch, little girl.
Make your fist sing its soft *goddamn*
smashing into the bridge of his nose.
He'll bob and weave, take out his clip
and whack it right into your skull. Don't cry.
Not even in the barracks. Not even now.

FIND HER BY THE FOUNTAIN

Hagar said to be a woman is to be
an immigrant. To be let in, briefly,
before being ushered out through the back.

To feel death's violent gaze and know
how to survive within it. To not iron out
the difference between sand

and sand. To be foreign, to be outside,
and know that it matters which passage
you press your ear to.

Pay when they demand.
Pay and pay and pay.
Pay with your children.

Say out loud, *I'm leaving.*
Even though you are an echo.
Even though no one asked.

THE DOVE THAT DIDN'T RETURN

The dove that didn't return to the ark
thought she'd have the world to herself.
She couldn't wait to fly off that floating
pile of wood planks, to escape the stench and the roaring.

She thought she'd have the world
to herself, but she immediately didn't.
There were dolphins and bottle-nosed whales
with strange calls, fish that never counted

water from water, microbes and organisms
writhing, multiplying in dark watery caves,
becoming in green and blue. On land,
the wind braided together the tiger grass,

the palms, the ginger's purple-tinted flowers
reaching toward the sun. She witnessed
the earth undusted—not a single footprint,
hoofprint, or rabbit pellet. No braying donkeys

or spider monkeys howling in trees.
The dove heard what silence was
and it was divine. It was just enough to bear.
She didn't have the world to herself

but she didn't want to own it.
She heard the sky alive with its breathing,
its give and take, its negotiation
with the desert mountain.

The dove didn't have the world to herself,
she knew, but she never returned
to report it. Maybe she thought
the ark couldn't store that kind of silence.

Maybe the story itself was
too large to carry back. Maybe, simply,
she saw through the glass
of the world and didn't want it to break.

II

AMOS 3:5

Of course, it wasn't the landmine's fault. The young couple parked
their car on the hem of the road. It was a wheat field. No, it was
barley. Wild and green stems swayed like birds in summer.
The oak promised some shade. She grabbed the picnic basket
from the car's trunk. There was an afternoon breeze, and the air
smelled of gravel. His handgun rested in the glove compartment.
It was quiet. They ducked under and through the wire-braided fence.
The yellow signs hung like lanterns. They spread the blanket, and
brought out the avocadoes, olive oil, black bread, pieces of cheese.
He was humming to himself an army chant from his nights
in the paratroopers, and she tucked a lose strand of her curls behind
her ear. When he stood, she caught a glint of something but didn't
know if it was sunlight. The cicadas didn't stop their clicking.
Not even the moment the white blast filled the sky.
The sound was metal itself fulfilling its position.
A plume of earth flowered open like a chute. It's possible
that he was so close to its break, he became the sound,
and she watched him become it. It's possible some migrant birds
ruptured the sky, briefly, before returning back to their perch.

TEFILLAT NE'ILAH

Ten days before Yom Kippur,
God's night of forgiveness, it's tradition
to ask it first of my kin.
My neighbors in the south
thirst on your lips lined with dust.
The homes you left in '48, I cemented shut;
they stand like brick ghosts of the banished.
Our father wronged us both, Ishmael,
but I have wronged you more.

TRADITION

We are just a family standing around a dinner table.
It's the sweetest hour of the evening, when
the day's leather has already begun to fade,
and my mother lights the Shabbat candles.

The gold flame dances and dips, and she waves
her hands over the low burn. My sisters and I
follow her circular gestures, as my father watches on.
We cover our eyes and speak silently with God.

We say, in those moments, what cannot be said aloud.
The air fills with fireflies. The evening perfumes
with fitna flowers and pomegranates.
Just before darkness, before the valley

of the shadow of death—there is here, there is this—
we stand around the dinner table, the six of us
like the braids of the Challa. When the Kiddush ends,
we will try to hold together for as long as we can.

FAMILIES OF THE EARTH

That night we hugged into our M-2 Bradley.
The war games were on their third day.

> We were all sleepless ghosts, shivering
> in our uniforms. It smelled distinctly of sweat

frozen and reheated, then frozen and reheated,
then frozen again. We were a fat pile of what was once

> men and women. Life at its worst
> and at its most beautiful.

We knew then, in a way that eludes me now,
that we were not dead.

> The rain hooded the clover field, and our Bradley
> metered through the mud.

The metal racket our battle bus made was more
than the crunch of basalt rock;

> it was the sudden puncture
> of love burrowing into the earth with its claws.

Trust me, It was not the only music we made.
We touched thighs, our helmets sleeted into

> each other, our shoulders grassed together,
> facing nothing but stars.

PEACE

Listen, even the olive tree
Needs to be beaten with a stick.

AN EYE FOR

The border, I tell you, is nothing but cement
taller and thicker than the olive trees around it.

And you should remember this when I tell you,
that the Israeli soldier said he fired because

he heard something in the distance. He said,
It sounded like a bullet; it sounded like a bark.

The man that was hurt, on the Lebanese side,
was a shepherd. And you should remember

that he had a gun on him at the time.
To kill wolves, he said.

And you are searching for a resolution;
or at least a language,

but I already told you,
the border is nothing but cement.

It cannot decide a bullet back into the cartridge.
It cannot tell a statement from the howling truth.

MORIAH

There was a ram lying on the ground.
      It was dead,
      but its legs looked like they were running.
A swarm of worms muzzled through its wool.

It had a curved knife stuck in its back — maybe
the ram ran a great distance before falling.
Maybe it ran backwards, into the knife.
      You had no way of knowing.

You weren't there when the ram became
      what dead things become.

Its skin was charred in some places, blacker
than the eye's iris. The regal horns still curled
onto themselves. The ram was fragrant
      with candelabra sage and ella leaves.

The ram did not spill out into the forest
or onto the knife. It contained itself.

You did what you thought you must:
      you backed away
      without turning your back.
As if to say to Abraham: This
was not what God had meant.

THE TAKING OF JERICHO

It happens when your nine-millimeter round
gets lodged in the chamber. I could be the dust, maybe,
or you just didn't put in the time to clean it.
No. It happens when you're sitting on the wooden chair
at the crowded café, waiting for the waitress
to bring over a salad, and you notice
that the tattooed birds on her wrist are flying away,
but you don't know where they're going. I say,
you notice the wrist but don't notice the man running in.
After he shoots, you want to shoot back,
but you didn't put in the time. And now you can't
get your breathing straight. You know
your handgun like you know Saturdays, like the number
seven. But you can't get that first bullet dislodged.
And you can't help but think of her sparrows
finally flocking, either north or south along the flyway.

THE GREAT ACHIEVEMENT OF
THE SIX DAY WAR

In the second before his tank
crawled onto a TM-38 mine,
Private Levi spotted three desert-colored helmets,
each a different height,
fleeing through a field of barley.

ODE TO THE FIELD

Green rye
swaying
in a field,
north and south
like a hammock
in soft wind,
will be ground
into flour,
into fresh bread,
into rugalach
for a woman,
and I could be
that woman
in my denim jacket
and blue cotton dress,
setting a picnic
on a beach
in Tel Aviv,
sipping Arak,
watching the sun's
last rays and your
wild laugh
and black hair
in the waves,
the same waves
you were buried under.
Your last words were:
Help me.
But all tides
are connected,

and after,
it was dark
and the waves
smelled different.
The water flows
back from Tel Aviv
into the rivers,
the river into streams,
and the streams
into irrigation
of those golden
green stems,
and now
it is almost as if
I can hear the rye.

DESIGNATION

Why should a word be a shield?
If anything, it drags me

back to the war.
The metal of my mind

rounded onto itself
like the 5.56 casing of an M-16 bullet.

When I stand in a rain field in January,
I align the sights of the riffle.

Shoot, my CO whispers.
I listen to my lungs fill and empty.

And I cannot pull the trigger
just to make it stop.

GOLIATH

The real tragedy of that cloudy day
took place when the eleven-foot man
watched a redhead boy running at him
with a wooden stick, an oversized coat of mail,
a helmet bobbing around loosely on his head.
And in a deep voice like a field,
he said to the boy, as only a father would,
Go home, son, just go home.
Goliath, he refused to believe
even when he finally saw the rock.

GHETTO WARSAW

David

Alone in the great chamber,
he is white haired and shivering,
like the snow that final May.
If he turns to dust,
who is left to deliver the psalms?

IF I FORGET YOU, JERUSALEM

As a bride, my mother wore a crown of fitna flowers.
Sometimes called red jasmine, the flower is neither
true red nor true jasmine.

Its rounded petals curl unto themselves, like delicate fingers
on the barrel of a gun. I love that the fire
hue spreads from its center but never reaches

the white edges, the way a bride opens into herself.
The botanist, Carl Linnaeus, called the blossom Plumeria Alba.
He classified the flowers as tapering and snowy white.

But in Arabic *fitna* means trial, strife, and burn.
The word stretches its thorns further than
the civil wars of the Khilāfah.

Semite traditions are always like this—
the lace overlay of paradox.
My mother is silent during the ceremony; she does

what brides do at their Chuppa.
But I love the way the fitna flowers after winter
like a celebration only beginning with the breaking of glass.

CHAVA

What was it she first saw
when she awoke on the hard ground?

The east wind blowing fig leaves,
petals from the garden,

dust and pollen, a bee's wing.
She must have unearthed her body

from itself. She must have named herself
not *Mother*, not *Eve*, but after

the evening primrose, the wild gull.
She must have seen the man

and his scarring, and knew
immediately he looked nothing like God.

CHAVA'S JUDGEMENT

She imagined herself, many years later,
straightening her eyes to God.
His beard of snakes and grime
was justice heavy and quivering.

He would have known, right then,
that he could not condemn her
to a life of governance.

He would have raised his eyes
to meet hers and remembered
that one heel was made for stomping
and one was made for stairs.

III

AHL AL-KITĀB

I teach my daughter the letter Aleph, with its one crooked
leg planted deep in the earth, like a cedar,
and its one arm outstretched toward the Torah.

She pours over the one letter, over and over.
Bishop wrote, "Nature repeats herself, or almost does:
repeat, repeat, repeat; revise, revise, revise."

I kneel beside my daughter over the low wooden table.
I kneel so that I can do the work of being beside.
The work of watching a child grow. Her long gold hair

falling forward, like a waterfall, spills onto the table like pools.
I watch her forehead curl inward like a closed fist.
Repeat, repeat, repeat; revise, revise, revise, revise.

SURGING WATERS STOOD
UP LIKE A WALL

When I was twenty and Ronny twenty-one,
the Northern War Room was alive with radio chatter.
>   *Sa'ar 5 is hit. Over.*
>   *C-802 anti-ship missile. Four dead.*
>   *Irretrievable. Lost at sea.*
My CO takes me outside the room,
sits me on a cheap white plastic chair.
It was the moment I knew,
even before the question appeared.

IRONSTONE

Red, like a sedimentary rock,
you lie in the river.
The shards of you forbid me
from recalling your face.

Bloated to the size of a cow
with the iron-muzzle broken:
the outline of your body
never did fit into your soul.

Your wild black hair
sunflower bleached,
bright yellow, almost white.
A vision of history

against the grain:
your eyes torn open,
as if you are remembering,
as if you are alive.

FIVE FATHOMS DEEP

—*after Marco Yan*

That summer rises
in me like

a tide, and I
am sanded to it.

I cannot return
to the wave

that shallowed
my friend.

I cannot ring the missel
back to its metaled nest.

And all that silence
cannot forgive me.

Like a grey stone
skipping three times

before it is shadowed
by the long dark—

my dead speaks
with the blue current

and his voice carries
me into that day.

GHETTO WARSHAW

Dear Moses, My Son

Tonight, I deliver you over the wall to another.
She will care for you, she will mother.
Remember that the city streets are seething with crocodiles,
their teeth like many crescent moons. Remember
who you are, remember us, please.

OF WOMEN IN THE TENT

Turn off the light! someone would bellow.
      Then the fireflies and tiger mosquitoes
run like messengers between our cots,
      humming their constellations of combat.
We are spent dry after a day of discipline,
      of marching, of perfect formations.
In the darkness, we rub our cherry
      bruises with coconut oil and menthol slims.
We unzip our kitbags, and like Pandora
      who loosened the great jar's lid,
out comes flying all manners of hell—
      tampons, energy bars, knockoff jasmine perfume,
phone-chargers coiled like thin white snakes.
      We tuck our M-16s under our pillows,
and someone, inevitably, caresses
      the rough of the pistol's grip.
Someone, inevitably, whispers too loudly
      and wakes up the guard.
Her tiny, scorpion-like eyes glow.
      In the darkness, we are all dangerous.
We rip at the seams, our serpent selves flying out.

WHAT I FORGOT FROM MY WARS

Let the night come & lay your head under
A blanket of dust. An orb of mosquitoes radios
Your position. Let them sing.

Even in the desert, the white capparis flowers
hold their stomachs as if they've been shot.
The larks of your mind are still cleaning, scrubbing.

Shooting is the cleaning of black oil into & out of.
You want to place your uniform on the shelf, one
sleeve at a time. Brush your hair into years.

You trace the outlines of your breath, as you
would a child's back. Say—it's safe now;
Say—I've got you. Let the night come

& lay your head under a blanket of dust.
 An orb of mosquitoes radios your position.
Let them sing. Hush your marching

& witness the constellation of canvas tents fill
with tens of girls in their cots, whispering to themselves
(or each other) the lullabies their mothers spoke.

I ONCE STOOD

in the great hall
of Bahad 1,
when I finished
Commander's Course.
It was a Friday
and the dust disappeared.
The air was not
yellow anymore
but light blue,
like how the wind
can stop screaming
for a moment,
and the world is still.
Except, on
that Friday—
the wind wasn't still.
It was screeching
and pulling,
the branches
from their scalps.
But the air,
the air was
light blue
or maybe clear.
In any case,
the day was warm.
It was warm
as if it remembered
all the things I
had to do to finish,

and was blushing.
As if it could recall,
the waiting
hour after hour
on the night watch,
and how I finished first
in navigation week.
How I tripped
and knocked loose
my front tooth.
And that misfire
my CO
kept screaming,
but the shot
went so close
to my ear,
I couldn't make out
a single word
he said.
It was always
dusty in that place,
but not that day.
That day,
I stood
amongst my peers
and my CO
pinned the pin
on my lapel
and I swear,
it must have been
I swear, it had to be
the clearest day
I've ever seen.

JULY IN NITZANIM TRAINING BASE

—enemy surveillance is to be conducted three hours a
day, in shifts of one.

An Agama lizard climbs from behind the boulders
concealed in yellow dust and hides in shade.
A hasty row of harvester ants searches for seeds,
find instead the edge of a pink tongue.
They shift only for a beat
before resuming formation.

COLLAPSED

My grandfather's
caretaker feeds him
one spoonful
at a time.
The sun
weaves through
the old oak.
I wonder
if it reminds
my grandfather
of the oak grove
in Nahalal,
shade stirring
the avocado tree,
the cow dung.
The whistle of boiling
water touches
thin glass
cups, green tea.
My grandfather's feet
are always in socks now.
What of the bare
soil, fallen branches,
beetles and black ants?
He can barely
move his hands,
granite stiff.
I remind myself
he was the 53 company
commander, and his

hands are the same
hands that once
carried his friend's
bullet-torn body
back to safety
between the trees.
How my grandfather
must have
collapsed then,
like a pinecone
toppling open
on the ground.

DELILAH

—after Yehuda Amichai

I remember a girl who crushed the legs of a dung beetle,
                    in the afternoon. The beetle was solemn as a
           cartridge of bullets.
Its dark body ascended slowly on the beach in Ashkelon like the last
of the judges.
The girl picked up a wooden stick and crushed its black legs.
                  She remembers she was a
                  soldier who watched her friend
                  get shot in the stomach.
How the friend remained standing, like a building with a rain
gutter,
                        the insides spilling out onto the street.
          The girl crushed the insect's legs, one at time.
              It was merciful. It was joyous.
The dung beetle was never alive until right then.

THIS WILL BE YOUR LAND
(WITH ITS BOUNDARIES ON EVERY SIDE)

—*after Mahmud Darwish*

I didn't tell you, but the radio chatter
from the field dispatch reported
that an olive tree broke.
   It wasn't the T-52 tank, they said.
It was nowhere near the thing.

The young tree broke from the lifted
dust, or from the weight of the day's
shadow. That's not important, they said.
   What's important is that the tree broke,
the way a tree breaks—splintered

from its stomach up, its large head bowed
in the direction of the Kaaba.
What's important is that the other trees
   weren't disturbed.
I've already told you everything else.

But the myna birds that were living
in the tree, fell to the sky. Screeching.
What they said to each other spread
   like a round of mortar,
like grief I've heard before.

THE GREAT ACHIEVEMENT OF
THE YOM KIPPUR WAR

The field is ignited as spring
& in it an abandoned tank
has gathered its wings,

its side skirt like barley.
& there I remember,
I'm standing on top of it.

Below me a field that smells
like carbon & steel & my father
is naming the different parts—

this is the T-72 barrel &
this is fire & these are daisies.
He says he remembers

the Syrians came from over
that hill and they sounded
nothing like defeat.

THE WESTERN WALL

I approach as if God
reads the notes yellowing in the cracks.

As if a wall can shield me
from a Sabbath rain,

like how a wall can swallow
a whole bullet and still

be a wall. And always
the four legs of the grey donkey

move together, unaware
of each other—

when I lean on the wall,
the wall leans back.

And still, it's a wall,
nothing more.

A place, like any other place,
to bang my head against and pray.

EXODUS

—after Najwan Darwish

I was a farmer from Nahalal.
I walked barefoot across the fields

if I could—between flights
of stairs if I could not.

Everywhere I went I was always
a grateful Russian who favored

good fortune and good health.
And I was a Pole, sitting in the shade

of an olive tree. I spread the napkin
evenly on my thighs, always looking

over my shoulder; even the Hermon's
snow could not erase 1942.

I was a proud Austrian,
I would not hesitate to throw a punch.

I was a white crane from Egypt,
spreading my wings in search of land.

I will not deny in every case
I was a Palestinian, among my sisters

who believe in the sword
and in the flag. I was a Jew,

looking within the corners of the letters
for the comfort of the sky.

Above all, I was an Israeli from Tzhala.
I heard the footsteps of my father, of his father,

of their fathers—and I will listen,
until I have something to say.

ABOUT THE AUTHOR

YAEL S. HACOHEN earned her Ph.D. at UC Berkeley. She has received research/teaching fellowships from Tel Aviv University and Bar Ilan University. She has an MFA in Poetry from New York University, where she was an NYU Veterans Workshop Fellow, International Editor at Washington Square Literary Review, and Editor-in-Chief at *Nine Lines Literary Review*. Her work has been featured or is forthcoming in *The Poetry Review, Ploughshares, The Missouri Review, Bellevue Literary Review, LIT, Prairie Schooner, New York Quarterly Magazine, Colorado Review*, and many more. Hacohen published her chapbook *Between Sanctity and Sand* with Finishing Line Press in 2021. Hacohen served as a lieutenant in the 162nd Armored Division of the Israeli Defense Forces. She lives with her family in Tel Aviv, Israel. For more information, please visit *www.yaelshacohen.com*

ACKNOWLEDGMENTS

I want to thank the editors of journals, magazines, and poetry competitions where my poems first appeared, sometimes in different forms and under different titles:

The Poetry Review, Prairie Schooner, Bellevue Literary Review, The Jewish Literary Journal, Consequence Magazine, LIT, Comstock Review, The Wrath-Bearing Tree, New York Quarterly Magazine, and *Nine Lines Review.*

The poem "Amos 3:5" won the Barbara Mandigo Kelly Peace Poetry Award.

Several of the poems in this collection appear in the chapbook "Between Sanctity and Sand," published in 2020 by Finishing Line Press.